# First World War
## and Army of Occupation
# War Diary
## France, Belgium and Germany

26 DIVISION
78 Infantry Brigade
Headquarters,
Princess Charlotte of Wales's
(Royal Berkshire Regiment) 7th Battalion,
Oxfordshire and Buckinghamshire Light Infantry
7th Battalion,
Gloucestershire Regiment 9th (Service) Battalion
and Worcestershire Regiment 11th Battalion
18 September 1915 - 31 October 1915

WO95/2253/2

The Naval & Military Press Ltd
www.nmarchive.com
**Published in association with The National Archives**

Published by

## The Naval & Military Press Ltd

Unit 10 Ridgewood Industrial Park,

Uckfield, East Sussex,

TN22 5QE England

Tel: +44 (0) 1825 749494

www.naval-military-press.com

www.nmarchive.com

*This diary has been reprinted in facsimile from the original. Any imperfections are inevitably reproduced and the quality may fall short of modern type and cartographic standards.*

© **Crown Copyright**
**Images reproduced by permission of The National Archives, London, England, 2015.**

# Contents

| Document type | Place/Title | Date From | Date To |
|---|---|---|---|
| Heading | WO95/2253/2 | | |
| Heading | 26th Division 78th Infy Bde Bde Headquarters 9th Bn Gloster Regt 11th Bn Worcester 7th Oxf & Bucks Lt Infy 7th Bn Berkshire Regt Sep-Oct 1915 | | |
| Heading | 26th Division 78th Inf. Bde. Vol I Sept To Oct 15 | | |
| War Diary | | 18/09/1915 | 31/10/1915 |
| Operation(al) Order(s) | Appendix 2 78th Inf. Bde Order No. 2 | 28/09/1915 | 28/09/1915 |
| Operation(al) Order(s) | Appendix 3 Operation Order No 2 | 28/09/1915 | 28/09/1915 |
| Operation(al) Order(s) | Appendix 5 78th Inf Bde Order No. 3 | 08/10/1915 | 08/10/1915 |
| Operation(al) Order(s) | Appendix 6 78th Infantry Brigade Order No. 4 | 21/10/1915 | 21/10/1915 |
| Miscellaneous | Ref. Amiens Sheet 12 1/80,000 | 21/10/1915 | 21/10/1915 |
| Miscellaneous | | 22/09/1915 | 22/09/1915 |
| Diagram etc | Appendix 7 | | |
| Operation(al) Order(s) | 5th Division Operation Order No. 70 | 29/09/1915 | 29/09/1915 |
| Miscellaneous | Appendix 4 Table Of Moves (Issued With 5th Division Operation Order No. 70) | | |
| Miscellaneous | 11th Batter Worcesteshire Regt | | |
| Miscellaneous | Time Table Attachment Of 7th. Oxfordshire & Buckinghamshire L.I. To 54th, Bde | | |
| Operation(al) Order(s) | 54th. Bde. Operation Order No. 8 | 29/09/1915 | 29/09/1915 |
| Heading | 26th Division 7th Berkshire Regt Vol I Sept Oct 15 | | |
| War Diary | Warminster | 19/09/1915 | 19/09/1915 |
| War Diary | Southampton Docks | 19/09/1915 | 19/09/1915 |
| War Diary | Havre | 20/09/1915 | 21/09/1915 |
| War Diary | Ailly Sur Somme | 22/09/1915 | 25/09/1915 |
| War Diary | Aubigny | 26/09/1915 | 29/09/1915 |
| War Diary | Albert | 30/09/1915 | 09/10/1915 |
| War Diary | Aubigny | 10/10/1915 | 22/10/1915 |
| War Diary | Bertangles | 23/10/1915 | 26/10/1915 |
| War Diary | Vignacourt | 27/10/1915 | 31/10/1915 |
| Heading | 26th Division 7th Ox & Bucks L.I. Vol I Sept Oct 15 | | |
| War Diary | Warminster | 19/09/1915 | 21/09/1915 |
| War Diary | Bologne | 22/09/1915 | 22/09/1915 |
| War Diary | Briquemesnil & Saisseval | 23/09/1915 | 24/09/1915 |
| War Diary | Ferrieres | 25/09/1915 | 25/09/1915 |
| War Diary | Fouilloy | 26/09/1915 | 29/09/1915 |
| War Diary | Meaulte & Becordel | 30/09/1915 | 09/10/1915 |
| War Diary | Fouilloy | 10/10/1915 | 18/10/1915 |
| War Diary | Laneuville | 19/10/1915 | 21/10/1915 |
| War Diary | Fouilloy | 22/10/1915 | 22/10/1915 |
| War Diary | Bertangles | 23/10/1915 | 31/10/1915 |
| Miscellaneous | Men Admitted To Hospital During Month Of October | | |
| Miscellaneous | Appendix I General Notes And Instructions As To Billeting Area Of 78th Infantry Brigade Group | | |
| Heading | 26th Division 9th G'cesters Vol I Sept 15 To Oct | | |
| War Diary | Sandhill Camp | 18/09/1915 | 28/09/1915 |
| Heading | 26th Division 11th Worcester Vol I Sept To Oct 15 | | |
| War Diary | Longbridge Deveril Wilts | 19/09/1915 | 19/09/1915 |
| War Diary | France | 21/09/1915 | 21/09/1915 |
| War Diary | Fourdrinoy | 22/09/1915 | 22/09/1915 |

| | | | |
|---|---|---|---|
| War Diary | Pont De Metz | 24/09/1915 | 24/09/1915 |
| War Diary | Fouilloy | 25/09/1915 | 28/09/1915 |
| War Diary | Sailly Lorette | 29/09/1915 | 30/09/1915 |
| War Diary | Maricourt And Suzanne | 01/10/1915 | 19/10/1915 |
| War Diary | Guzanne And Sailly | 07/10/1915 | 07/10/1915 |
| War Diary | Lorette | 08/10/1915 | 08/10/1915 |
| War Diary | Fouilloy | 09/10/1915 | 17/10/1915 |
| War Diary | Framerville & Vauvillers | 18/10/1915 | 21/10/1915 |
| War Diary | Vaux-En-Amienois | 22/10/1915 | 31/10/1915 |

WO 95/22513 (2)

WO 95/22513 (2)

26TH DIVISION
78TH INFY BDE

BDE HEADQUARTERS
9TH BN GLOSTER REGT
11TH BN WORCESTER ..
7TH OXF. & BUCKS LT INFY
7TH BN BERKSHIRE REGT

SEP - OCT 1915

26th Kirwin

$\frac{12}{7431}$

78½ Sept. Bde:
rot I & II

Sept 1 & Oct 15

Army Form C. 2118

# WAR DIARY
## or
## INTELLIGENCE SUMMARY
*(Erase heading not required.)*

Instructions regarding War Diaries and Intelligence Summaries are contained in F. S. Regs., Part II. and the Staff Manual respectively. Title Pages will be prepared in manuscript.

| Place | Date | Hour | Summary of Events and Information | Remarks and references to Appendices |
|---|---|---|---|---|
| | 18th. Sept. | | 7th.Royal Berks Regt. and Transport of the Brigade left LONGBRIDGE DEVERILL for HAVRE via SOUTHAMPTON arriving HAVRE 7-30 a.m. 19th. | All references must to plan work Sheets 12 & 13 (AMIENS & CAMBRAI) 1/80000 |
| | 19th. Sept. | | 7th. Royal Berks. Regt. and Transport of Brigade in HAVRE. Headquarters Transport move to Billets by Rail near AMIENS. | |
| | 20th. Sept. | | 7th.Royal Berks Regt. by Rail to AILLY (near AMIENS.) | |
| | 21st. Sept. | | Headquarters Personnel and Personnel of 11th.Worc.Regt., 9th.Glouc.Regt. and 7th.Ox & Bucks L.I. left LONGBRIDGE DEVERILL and Railed at various hours from 3-20 p.m. onwards to FOLKESTONE thence BOULOGNE. | |
| | 22nd. Sept. | | Personnel of Brigade (less Royal Berks Regt) arrived BOULOGNE 12-20 a.m. Brigade commenced entraining for SALEUX near AMIENS. During the afternoon and night, all Units arrived and were billeted, in FERRIERES (Headquarters and Signal Section) 9th.Glouc.Regt. FOURDRINOY, 11th.Worc.Regt. BRIQUEMESNIL, SAISSEVAL, SAISSEMINT, 7th.Ox & Bucks L.I.; AILLY 7th.Royal Berks Regt. In addition came under Brigade Orders the 108th.Field Coy., billeted at ST.CHRIST FARM and 78th.Field Ambulance at AILLY. | App. I |
| | 23rd. Sept. | | All troops rested in billets. ~~Further orders~~ | |
| | 24th. Sept. | | 11th.Worc.Regt. were brought in from FOURDRINOY to FERRIERES and then ordered to PONT DE METZ, in anticipation of a long march East on the 25th. The 7th.Ox & Bucks L.I. arrived at FERRIERES from BRIQUEMESNIL and billeted in the former. General MUNRO, Commanding 3rd.Army inspected the 7th. Ox & Bucks L.I. and 9th.Glouc.Regt. at 4-30 p.m. Received orders for a move on 25th. | |
| | 25th. Sept. | | The Brigade marched to new Billets at FOUILLOY and AUBIGNY distance 17½ miles. In the Brigade Group were also 114th. and 115th. F.A.Bdes. and 108th.Field Coy. March was witnessed at different points by the 3rd.Corps Commander (Sir Henry Wilson) and the Divisional Commander. | |
| | 26th. Sept. | | All Units rested in Billets and cleaned up equipment. | |

Army Form C. 2118.

# WAR DIARY
## or
## INTELLIGENCE SUMMARY.
*(Erase heading not required.)*

Instructions regarding War Diaries and Intelligence Summaries are contained in F.S. Regs., Part II. and the Staff Manual respectively. Title pages will be prepared in manuscript.

| Place | Date | Hour | Summary of Events and Information | Remarks and references to Appendices |
|---|---|---|---|---|
| | 27th. Sept. | | All Battalions carried out Battalion Training throughout the day, with special reference to "open fighting". A Machine Gun Course for 8 Officers in the Brigade was formed and is to commence work tomorrow. Other troops billeted in the Brigade Area and under the Brigadier General, Commanding 78th.Infantry Brigade for discipline in billets and rations are 114th., 115th., 117th. Field Artillery Brigades, 108th.Field Coy., 78th.Field Ambulance. | |
| | 28th. Sept. | | Battalion training for all Units. Lieut.Colonel R.E.T.Bray, 7th.Royal Berks Regt: handed over Command to Major Sexton, the former being placed on the sick list. The Brigade is ordered to break up for Training in Trench Routine as follows:-<br>9th.Glouc.Regt. attached to 5th.Division and ordered to billet at CHIPILLY.<br>11th.Worc.Regt. attached to 5th.Division and ordered to billet at SAILLY LORETTE.<br>7th.Ox & Bucks L.I. attached to 18th.Division and ordered to billet at MEAULTE.<br>7th.Royal Berks Regt. attached to 18th.Division and ordered to billet at ALBERT. | |
| | 29th. Sept. | | The moves ordered in the afternoon of the 28th. took place (see Operation Order No.2 & 2(a)). Brigade Headquarters remained at FOUILLOY. It was definitely arranged that Units should be attached for training in the trenches to the following Brigades:-<br>9th.Glouc.Regt. to 15th.Infantry Brigade, Headquarters at BRAY.<br>11th.Worc.Regt. to 14th.Infantry Brigade, Headquarters at SUZANNE.<br>7th.Ox & Bucks L.I. to 54th.Infantry Brigade, Headquarters at MEAULTE.<br>7th.Royal Berks Regt. to 53rd.Infantry Brigade, Headquarters at ALBERT. | App. 2 y 3 |
| | 30th. Sept. | | 78th.Infantry Brigade Headquarters and No.3 Signal Section moved to SAILLY LORETTE. On same date 9th.Glouc.Regt. marched from CHIPILLY to CARNOY, BILLON FM. and BRONFAY FM. Two Companies of the 11th.Worc.Regt. marched from SAILLY LORETTE to SUZANNE. Both these moves being preparatory to entering the trenches. Brigadier General visited H.Q. of 5th Division. | |
| | 1st. Oct. | | Units of the Brigade commenced instruction in Trench Routine as per attached programmes. The Brigadier General visited Headquarters 18th.Division, 53rd. and 54th. Infantry Brigades. Brigade Major and Brigade Machine Gun Officer visited Headquarters 14th. and 15th. Infantry Brigades. | App. 4 |

Army Form C. 2118.

# WAR DIARY
## or
## INTELLIGENCE SUMMARY.
*(Erase heading not required.)*

Instructions regarding War Diaries and Intelligence Summaries are contained in F.S. Regs., Part II. and the Staff Manual respectively. Title pages will be prepared in manuscript.

| Place | Date | Hour | Summary of Events and Information | Remarks and references to Appendices |
|---|---|---|---|---|
| | 1st. to 8th. Oct. | | Units were attached for instruction to 5th. and 18th.Divisions as follows:- 9th.Glouc.Regt. to 15th.Brigade.) 5th.Division. The 15th.Inf.Bde. handed over to the 13th. 11th.Worc.Regt. to 14th.Brigade.) 7th.Ox & Bucks L.I. to 54th.Brigade. ) 18th. Division. 7th.Royal Berks Regt. to 53rd.Brigade.) The trenches of each Battalion were visited by the Brigadier General in turn. The casualties during this period of attachment were unusually heavy.     9th.Glouc.Regt.   11th.Worc.Regt   7th.Ox & Bucks L.I.   7th.Royal Berks Regt.     Killed   Wounded   Killed   Wounded   Killed   Wounded   Killed   Wounded     2   1   nil   4 (1 Off.)   11   32 (1 Off.)   nil   nil | App.s |
| | 9th. Oct. | | The Brigade reassembled in billets in FOUILLOY and AUBIGNY. | |
| | 10th. Oct. | | A day spent in billets resting. Battalions all went through a gas helmet test, under the supervision of the 3rd.Army Chemical Advisor. Gas was produced from a cylinder and Units marched through it, with helmets on. | |
| | 11th. to 13th. Oct. | | Training re-commenced on the lines laid down before the Brigade moved to the trenches of the 5th. and 18th.Divisions for instruction. | |
| | 14th. Oct. | | The 9th.Glouc.Regt. marched E. to MORCOURT in the 27th.Divisional Area to work on the Corps line of trenches which is being prepared on a line N and S and just E of that place. The Battalion is being accommodated in a camp pitched near MORCOURT wood. The 11th.Worc.Regt. was under orders to proceed to the vicinity of the same place, but is detained by lack of water in the neighbourhood of proposed camp. | |
| | 15th. to 17th. Oct. | | The Brigade less 9th.Glouc.Regt. continued training. | |
| | 18th. Oct. | | The 11th.Worc.Regt. marched at 9 a.m. to FRAMERVILLE and VAUVILLERS to work on Corps 2nd.Line of defence. 7th.Ox & Bucks L.I. marched at 9-30 a.m. to LAMEUVILLE (Near BRAY) also to work on the above line of defence. | |
| | 19th. Oct. | | Nil. | |

Army Form C. 2118.

# WAR DIARY
## or
## INTELLIGENCE SUMMARY.
*(Erase heading not required.)*

Instructions regarding War Diaries and Intelligence Summaries are contained in F. S. Regs., Part II. and the Staff Manual respectively. Title pages will be prepared in manuscript.

| Place | Date | Hour | Summary of Events and Information | Remarks and references to Appendices |
|---|---|---|---|---|
| | 20th. Oct. | | Orders received for the concentration of the Brigade in its Billets at FOUILLOY and AUBIGNY by the 21st.with a view to evacuating our billeting area by the 22nd. to make room for the French who are taking over all trenches S of the River Somme. The reason for this alteration of existing dispositions is to be found in the necessity for the despatch of troops from France to SALONIKA. | |
| | 21st. Oct. | | The Brigade concentrated today at FOUILLOY and AUBIGNY. 9th.Glouc.Regt. arrived 12-20 p.m. from MORCOURT distance 9 miles. 11th.Worc.Regt. arrived 1-30 p.m. from FRAMERVILLE and VAUVILLERS, distance 12½ miles. 7th. Ox & Bucks L.I. arrived 4-30 p.m. from LANEUVILLE (Near BRAY) distance 13½ miles. | App. 6. |
| | 22nd. Oct. | | The Brigade marched to its new billeting area N of AMIENS. Hour of start 8-30 a.m. All Units reported settled in billets by 4-30 p.m. as follows:- <br> Headquarters and 7th.Ox & Bucks L.I.) BERTANGLES. <br> 7th.Royal Berks Regt) <br> 9th.Glouc.Regt. at MONTONVILLERS. <br> 11th.Worc.Regt. at VAUX en AMIENOIS. | |
| | 23rd. Oct. 24th. Oct. | | The day was devoted to cleaning up Billets and resting. The 102nd French Mortar Bty was attached in Brig hdqts by the Bde, & was billeted at MONTONVILLERS. <br> Church parades were held in Battalion billets. | |
| | 25th. Oct. | | Orders were received at 12-10 a.m. for Headquarters and 1 Battalion to evacuate Billets at BERTANGLES, leaving there only one Battalion. The Staff Captain proceeded to RAINNEVILLE and VIGNACOURT reconnoitering for Billets. These were found and allotted at 12 noon as follows:- Brigade Headquarters to FREMONT. 7th.Royal Berks Regt. to VIGNACOURT. At 7-25 a.m. the same day, the Brigadier General ordered a test alarm. Units to assemble by 11 a.m. at the Brigade Alarm Post, at the Cross Roads just W of the B of BERTANGLES. This was satisfactorily carried out, all Units assembling with Transport complete and ready to march away. Other troops in the Brigade Area who carried out the test were the 108th.Field Coy., 78th.Field Ambulance, and No.3 Coy.Train. | App. 7. |
| | 26th. to 31st Oct. | | The Brigade continued its training. No movements took place during this period. | |

Sc. Thomas, Br/Gnl Cmd'g 70th Infy Bde
31.10.15.

APPENDIX 2

78th Inf. Bde. Order No. 2
28-9-15

1. The 9/Glouc. R. and 11th Worc. R. will march tomorrow to SAILLY LORETTE and CHIPILLY
   Starting point: Junc. Bridge between CORBIE & FOUILLOY
   Time: 10 a.m.
   Route: HAMELET – ~~VAIRE SOUS CORBIE~~ CORBIE – VAUX SUR SOMME – SAILLY LE SEC.
   Order of march:
       9/Glouc. R.
       11/Worc. R.
       "B" echelon 1st line Trans. (both units)
       Train (in same order of march as units)

2. Billetting parties must reach both destinations by 11 am (Div. letter G.75 has been amended.)

3. Supply wagons will join units at the starting point.

R. O. Marsland, Maj.
OBM
78th Inf. Bde.

Issued at 8 pm. Is
9/Glouc. Copy 1
11/Worc. " 2
File " 3

# APPENDIX 3

Operation Order No. 2 (a)
28-9-15

1. The 7/Ox & Bucks L.I. and 7/R. Berks R. will march tomorrow to MEAULTE and ALBERT. The 7/Ox & Bucks L.I. will halt & billet at MEAULT, the 7/BERKS at ALBERT.

Starting pt: 7/Ox. Bucks L.I. the Bde. H.Q.

Time: 9.30 am.

Starting pt: 7/R. Berks R. the Eastern exit of AUBIGNY

Time: 9 am.

Route: CORBIE - MERICOURT - VILLE SUR ANCRE - MEAULT.

Order of march
 7/Ox & Bucks L.I.
 7/Berks R.
 "B" echelon, 1st line Trans (Bde units)
 Train (in order of march of units)

2. Supply wagons will meet both units at FOUILLOY CHURCH & join the train.

Thos Hankin Maj
Bde.
78th L Bde.

Issued at 8.15 pm
7/Ox & Bucks copy 1
7/R. Berks R.  " 2
file  " 3

APPENDIX 5

78th Inf. Bde. Order No 3      Copy 3

8-10-15

Ref. sheet AMIENS
(17) 1/80.000

1. The 9/Glouc. R. & 1/Worc. R. will return to their billets at FOUILLOY tomorrow the 9th as below:—

|  | S. Pt. | Time | Route |
|---|---|---|---|
| 1/Worc. R. | Western end of SAILLY LORETTE | 10.30 am | SAILLY LE SEC – VAUX S. SOMME – CORBIE. |
| 9/Glouc. R. | N.W. end of CHIPILLY | 10 am |  |

1/Worc. R

2. Col. Rainey-Robinson C.B., 1/Worc.R. will command the column.

3. Billetting parties of both units will precede their Bns. by 3 hours and arrange to re-occupy their former billets.

4. Reports to head of 1/Worc. R.

Issued at 3.30 p.m.          Ren. S Maitland Maj.
to.                                   Bn. 78th Inf. Bde.
1/Worc. R.   Copy 1
9/Glouc. R.    " 2
file               " 3

APPENDIX 6.

## 78th INFANTRY BRIGADE ORDER No.4
### 21:10:15

1. The 78th. Infantry Brigade Group marches to new billets tomorrow at BERTANGLES, MONTONVILLERS and VAUX en AMIENOIS as below :-

| Unit | Starting Point | Hour | Route | Remarks |
|---|---|---|---|---|
| H.Q.78th.Inf. Bde. & Sig. Section | CORBIE BRIDGE | 8-30 a.m. | PONT NOYELLES- QUERRIEUX-ALLON- VILLE-COISY | |
| 11th.Worc.R. | do. | 8-30 a.m. | | ) Leave column |
| 9th.Glouc.R. | do. | 8-35 a.m. | | ) of route at |
| 7th.Ox & Bucks L.I. | do. | 8-40 a.m. | | ) BERTANGLES |
| 7th.R.Berks.R | E.exit of AUBIGNY | 8-20 a.m. | | |
| B.Echelon 1st.Line Tpt. | | 8-50 a.m. | | |
| No.7 Coy. Train | CORBIE BRIDGE | 9-0 a.m. | | |
| 78th.Field Ambulance | | 9-10 a.m. | | |

2. (a) echelon 1st.Line Transport of Infantry Units to follow each Unit.
   (b) echelon to be in order of march of units.

   The Brigade Transport Officer to be at CORBIE BRIDGE at 8-50 a.m. to marshall (b) echelon 1st.Line Transport.

3. Baggage Wagons will be sent to Battalion Billets by O.C. Train at 3 a.m.
   Blanket Wagons supplied by the Division, arrive at Brigade Headquarters, FOUILLOY at 7 a.m. Guides from Units will conduct them to Battalion Billets.

4. Refilling Point for 78th. Brigade Group on 23rd. at Cross Roads ½ mile W. of COISY at 7-30 a.m. and 3-30 p.m.

5. Reports to Head of Column.

                                            Major
                                       Brigade Major
                                    78th Infantry Brigade

Issued at      p.m.

To   9th.Glouc.Regt.    Copy 1
     11th.Worc.Regt.     "   2
     7th.Ox & Bucks L.I. "   3
     7th.R.Berks R.      "   4
     78th.Fd.Amb.        "   5
     No.7 Coy.Train      "   6
     Bde.Transp.Officer  "   7
     H.Q.            Copies 8 to 10

Subject :- Move.    Ref. AMIENS Sheet 12    1/80,000

To O.C.

    th.

                                            21st October 1915

The Brigade moves to new billets North of AMIENS tomorrow, and will be distributed on its arrival there as follows:-

H.Q. 78th. Inf. Bde.  )
7th. Ox & Bucks L.I.  )    BERTANGLES
7th. Royal Berks Regt.)

9th. Glouc. Regt.     )
108th. Field Coy.     )    MONTONVILLERS

11th. Worc. Regt.     )
No.3 Coy. Train.      )    VAUX-en-AMIENOIS
78th. Field Amb.      )


Billeting parties of the above units will assemble at Brigade Headquarters by 6 a.m. tomorrow where they will be met by the Staff Captain and the whole party will move off together.

Billeting parties must be mounted on cycles or horses. Orders for the march of the Brigade have not yet been received, but it is anticipated that the hour of start will be about 8 a.m.

                                    [signature]
                                        Major
                                    Brigade Major
                                    78th Infantry Brigade.


3-50 p.m.

7. **Billeting parties.** Billeting parties will march at head of column. on arrival in units billeting area the Billeting Officer will proceed to the mayors office (La Mairie) and get the list of billets and allot, ~~refferin~~ referring for particulars of his unit's area to instructions to Billeting Officer.

8. **Water.** The water throughout the area (except at AILLY) is very bad and very scarce. Men should not be allowed to drink any water that has not been boiled or treated chemically. The village ponds are probably too dirty even for animals to drink from, (sentries should be posted _if necessary_ to prevent men drinking from them.) Special notes as to water in each area will be found in Instruction to Billeting Officer.

9. **Transport & Animals.** Transport will be parked and animals picketed in any adjacent field that has not crops on it.

10. **Cafes.** Cafes are open for troops from 11am to one pm and six pm to eight pm.

11. **Fire.** AS many of the billets are in farms etc: the danger of fire is considerable and no smoking should be permitted where there is any danger of fire.

12. The Refilling Point is at the cross roads marked "R" on map ~~due~~ east of FOURDRINOY; times for drawing supplies will be notified by Supply Officer to each unit as soon as possible after arrival.

T.H. Keary
Lt
Staff Capt'n
78th Inf Bde.

Chateau de Ferrieres
22/9/15.

_Reference 7 above, your transport has arrived + necessary billeting has been done_

APPENDIX 7.

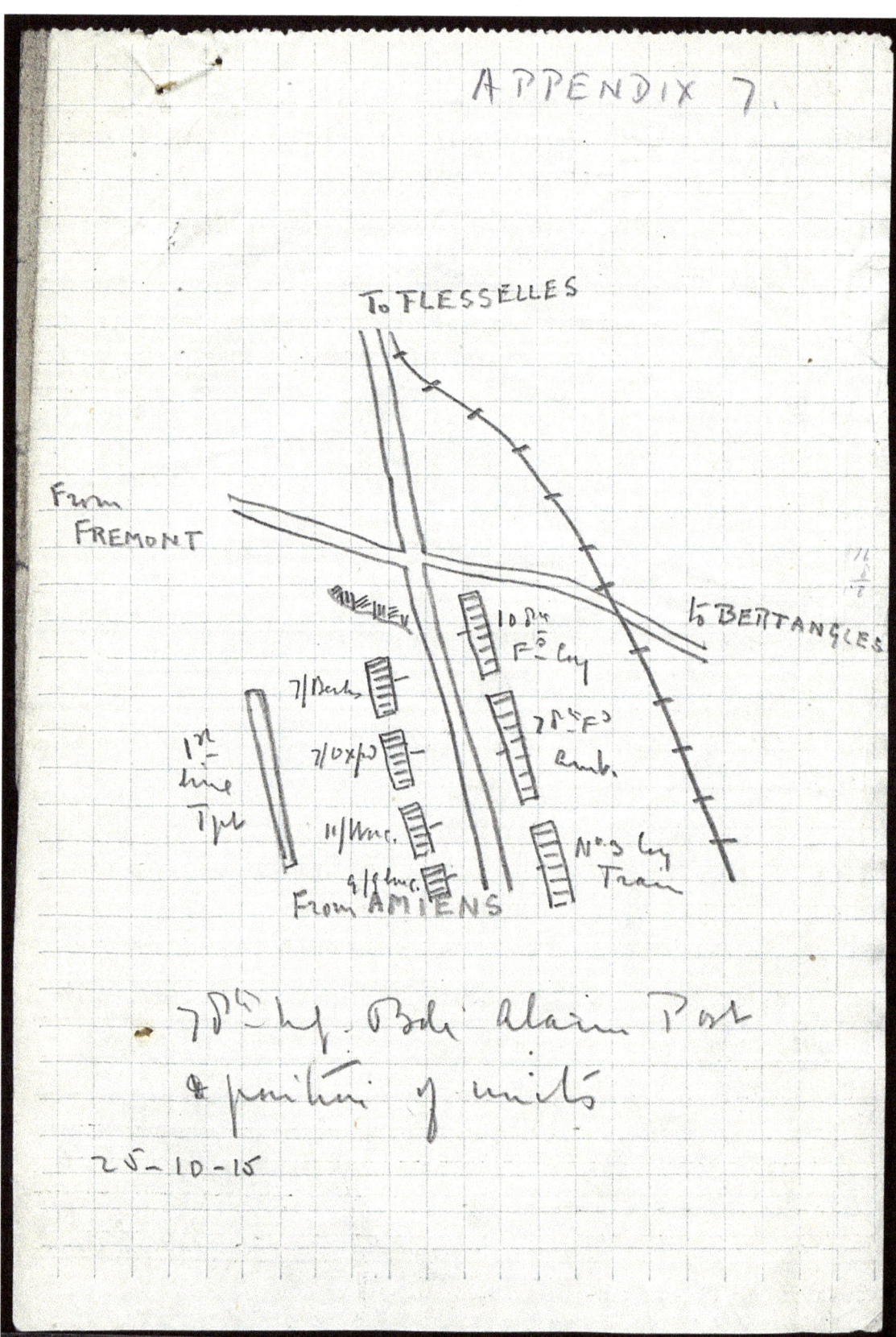

7th Div. Bde Alarm Post
& positions of units

25-10-15

## 5th Division Operation Order No. 70

29th September 1915.

1. The 9th Bn. Gloucester Regiment and 11th Bn. Worcester Regiment will be attached to 5th Division for training in trench warfare from 29th instant.

2. From 30th instant, the 9th Bn. Gloucester Regiment will be attached to the 15th Infantry Brigade for training in "B" Sector, and 11th Bn. Worcester Regiment to the 14th Infantry Brigade for training in "A" Sector.

3. Training to be carried out in accordance with 10th Corps G.S. 60, forwarded to Infantry Brigades with 5th Division G.B. 562 dated September 7th.

4. The 26th Division will arrange to ration these battalions during their attachment to 5th Division.

5. O.C. 9th Bn. Gloucester Regiment will report himself at 15th Infantry Brigade Headquarters at BRAY at 9 a.m. on 30th instant, and O.C. 11th Bn. Worcester Regiment at Divisional Headquarters EINQUIN at the same hour.

6. Two guides from 5th Divisional Cyclist Company will report to 9th Bn. Gloucester Regiment at 9 a.m. on 30th, and two guides to 11th Bn. Worcester Regiment at 9 a.m. on September 30th and October 1st.

7. Table of moves is attached.

Lt.Colonel,
General Staff, 5th Division.

Issued at 9 a.m.

10th Corps
12th Corps.
26th Division.
73th Inf. Bde. (3 copies)
13th " "
14th " "
15th " "
5th Division "Q".
Div. Cyclist Company.

# APPENDIX 4.

## TABLE OF MOVES. (Issued with 5th Division Operation Order No. 70).

| Date | Unit | From | To | Remarks. |
|---|---|---|---|---|
| Sept. 29th/30th. | 9th Bn. Glouc. R. | FOUILLOY | CHIPILLY. | Billeting party meets Staff Officer, 5th Div. at CHIPILLY Church at 11 a.m. 29th. |
| " | 11th Bn. Worc. R. | FOUILLOY | SAILLY LORETTE | Billeting party meets Staff Officer, 5th Div. at SAILLY LORETTE Church 11.30 a.m. 29th. |
| Sept. 30th/Oct.1st. | 9th Bn. Glouc. R. | CHIPILLY | CARNOY, BRONFAY and BILLON Wood. | Half Officers and N.C.O's to trenches of 'B' sector. |
| " | 2 Companies 11th Bn. Worc. R. | SAILLY LORETTE | SUZANNE | Officers and N.C.O's of these 2 companies will go into trenches that night. They will be sent to SUZANNE by motor bus in afternoon if it can be arranged. |
| " | 9th Bn. London R. | CARNOY and BRONFAY. | CHIPILLY | Remaining half Officers and N.C.O's to trenches. |
| " | 9th Bn. Glouc. R. | SUZANNE | Trenches. | |
| Oct. 1st/2nd. | 2 Companies 11th Bn. Worc.R. | SAILLY LORETTE | SUZANNE | |
| " | 2 Companies 9th Glouc. R. | CARNOY | Trenches | |
| Oct. 2nd/3rd. | 1 Company each from 1st Chesh. R. and 1st Dorset R. | Trenches | CARNOY | |

## Table of moves (continued).

| Date | Unit | From | To | Remarks. |
|---|---|---|---|---|
| October 3rd/4th. | | | | During nights 2nd/3rd and 3rd/4th remaining officers and N.C.O's 11th Bn. Worcester Regiment do their tour in trenches half at a time. |
| 4th/5th. | 2 Coys. 11th Worc. R. | Trenches | SUZANNE | |
| | 2 Cos. 11th Worc R | SUZANNE | Trenches. | |
| 5th/6th. | 2 Cos. 9th Glouc. R. | Trenches | BRONFAY and BILLON | |
| | 2 Cos. 9th Glouc. R. | BRONFAY and BILLON | Trenches. | |
| 7th/8th. | 2 Cos. 11th Worc. R. | Trenches | SUZANNE | |
| | 2 Cos. 11th Worc. R. | SUZANNE | SAILLY LORRAINE. | |
| 8th/9th. | 9th London Regt. | CHIPILLY | 13th Bde. area. | |
| " | 9th Glouc. R. | Trenches and BRONFAY | CHIPILLY. | |
| " | 2 Cos. 11th Worc. R. | SUZANNE | SAILLY LORRAINE. | |
| 9th. | Battalions return to command of their Divisions. | | | |

11th Battn: Worcestershire Regt.

| Distribution | 24 Hours. Individual. | | 48 Hours. as Platoons. | | 24 Hours. as Companies. | | Attached To. | Remarks |
|---|---|---|---|---|---|---|---|---|
| | From: | To: | From: | To: | From: | To: | | |
| Officers and NCOs A. Coy. A. Coy. | 6 pm Sept. 30th | 6 pm Oct 1st | 7 pm Oct 1st | 7 pm Oct 3rd | 7 pm Oct 3rd | 7 pm Oct 4th | 5th Cheshires. | |
| Officers and NCOs B. Coy. B. Coy. | - do - | - do - | - do - | - do - | - do - | - do - | D.C.L.I. | |
| Officers, NCOs C. Coy. " " C. Coy. | 6 pm Oct 2nd 6 pm Oct 3rd | 6 pm Oct 3rd 6 pm Oct 4th | 7 pm Oct 4th | 7 pm Oct 6th | 7 pm Oct 6th | 7 pm Oct 7th | 5th Cheshires. | |
| Officers & NCOs D. Coy. " " D. Coy. | - do - | - do - | - do - | - do - | - do - | - do - | D.C.L.I. | |

F. Phillips Major
Brigade Major.

## TIME TABLE.

Attachment of 7th. Oxfordshire & Buckinghamshire L.I. to 54th. Bde.

| Date. | Time. | Coy. | Attached to | Sector. | Instruction. | Remarks. |
|---|---|---|---|---|---|---|
| Sept. 30th. | 3 p.m. | W. | 6th. Bn. North'n. R. | D.1. | 24 hours individual instruction Officers and N.C.O's. only. | (1) Parties will reach Bn.H.Q. of Bn. in trenches at hour named. |
| 30th. | 3 p.m. | X. | 12th. Bn. Midd'x. R. | D.2. | ditto. | |
| Oct. 1st. | 3 p.m. | W. | 6th. Bn. North'n. R. | D.1. | 48 hours Platoon instruction, Platoons being employed as such. | (2) Guides from Bn. in trenches will report at Bde. Hd. Qrs. at 1.30 p.m. daily, and will be sent to Bn. Hd. Qrs. Oxon & Bucks L.I. to guide parties. |
| 1st. | 3 p.m. | X. | 12th. Bn. Midd'x. R. | D.2. | ditto. | |
| 3rd. | 3 p.m. | Y. | 6th. Bn. North'n. R. | D.1. | 24 hours Individual instruction Officers and N.C.O's only. | (3) In case of relief of a Bn. of 54th. Bde. by another Bn. of same Bde. during period of attachment, the programme may have to be altered. |
| 3rd. | 3 p.m. | Z. | 12th. Bn. Midd'x. R. | D.2. | ditto. | |
| 4th. | 3 p.m. | Y. | 6th. Bn. North'n. R. | D.1. | 48 hours platoon instruction, platoons as such. | |
| 4th. | 3 p.m. | Z. | 12th. Bn. Midd'x. R. | D.2. | ditto. | |
| 6th. | 3 p.m. | W. | 6th. Bn. North'n. R. | D.1. | 24 hours Coy. instruction, Coys. being employed as such. | |
| 6th. | 3 p.m. | X. | 12th. Bn. Midd'x. R. | D.2. | ditto. | |
| 7th. | 3 p.m. | Y. | 6th. Bn. North'n. R. | D.1. | ditto. | |
| 7th. | 3 p.m. | Z. | 12th. Bn. Midd'x. R. | D.2. | ditto. | |

Copy No. 5

## 54th. Bde. Operation Order No. 8.

29th. September, 1915.

1. The 7th. Bn. Oxfordshire and Buckinghamshire Light Infantry will be attached to the 54th. Bde. from 29th. September for induction. Hd. Qrs. and 2 Coys. will be billeted at MEAULTE, 2 Coys. at BECORDEL, and Transport at MEAULTE.

2. When platoons are attached to Coys. or Coys. to Bns. in the trenches, platoon or Coy. Commanders of the 7th. Bn. Oxon & Bucks L.I. will take their orders from the Coy. or Bn. to which they are attached.

3. Parties of the 7th. Oxon & Bucks L.I., when in trenches, will be rationed by their own Battalion, rations being sent up at night with rations of Bn. to which they are attached. The Wagons with rations, etc., must move with those of Bn. in trenches.

4. O.C. and Adjutant of 7th. Oxon & Bucks L.I. will visit Hd. Qrs., of 6th. Bn. North'n. R. and 12th. Bn. Midd'x. R, on 30th. September and arrange any details necessary.

5. Companies will go into trenches in accordance with attached Table.

(Signed) M. Hore-Ruthven, Major,
Bde. Major,
54th. Bde.

Issued at 2.30 p.m.

Copy No. 1. Office.
2. 7th. Oxon & Bucks L.I.
3. 6th. Bn. North'n. R.
4. 12th. Bn. Midd'x. R.
5. 18th. Div.
6. Spare.

18/36th Division

7th Berkshire Rgt.
vol: I & II

Sept & Oct 15

D/
7431

Army Form C. 2118.

# WAR DIARY
## INTELLIGENCE SUMMARY.
*(Erase heading not required.)*

Instructions regarding War Diaries and Intelligence Summaries are contained in F. S. Regs., Part II. and the Staff Manual respectively. Title pages will be prepared in manuscript.

| Place | Date | Hour | Summary of Events and Information | Remarks and references to Appendices |
|---|---|---|---|---|
| WARMINSTER | 19.9.15 | 5.55a– 7.25am 8.55am | Battalion entrained and proceeded by rail to SOUTHAMPTON DOCKS. | 1 Tnk |
| SOUTHAMPTON DOCKS | 19.9.15 | 7.0 pm | Embarked | 1 Tnk |
| HAVRE | 20.9.15 | 7.0 am | Disembarked. Proceeded to No 5. Rest Camp. | 1 Tnk |
| " | 21.9.15 | 1.15pm | Proceeded by rail to LONGUEAU, on arrival there by route march to AILLY-SUR-SOMME and billeted there | 1 off. to G.S. 1 off. to Base 1 off. to G.S. |
| AILLY-SUR-SOMME | 22.9.15 | | } Nothing to report | 1 Tnk 1 Tnk 1 Tnk |
| " | 23.9.15 | | | |
| " | 24.9.15 | | | |
| " | 25.9.15 | 9.0 am | Proceeded by route march to AUBIGNY and billeted there | 1 Tnk 1 Tnk |
| AUBIGNY | 26.9.15 | | } Nothing to report | 1 Tnk 1 Tnk |
| " | 27.9.15 | | | |
| " | 28.9.15 | | 1st Lt R.E.T. BRAY placed on sick list. Major J.T.O'B SEXTON took over command. | 10 pm M guard |
| " | 29.9.15 | 9.0 am | Proceeded by route march to ALBERT for attachment to 53rd Brigade, 18th Division for tuition in trench warfare. | 1 Tnk 1 Tnk |
| ALBERT | 30.9.15 | | Officers & Platoon Sergeants reconnoitred trenches | 1 Tnk |

Army Form C. 2118.

# WAR DIARY
## or
## INTELLIGENCE SUMMARY.
(Erase heading not required.)

| Place | Date | Hour | Summary of Events and Information | Remarks and references to Appendices |
|---|---|---|---|---|
| ALBERT | 1.10.15 | | A & B Companies attached to 10th Essex and C & D to 8th Suffolk Battalions for instruction in trench warfare | |
| " | 2.10.15 | | nothing to report | |
| " | 3.10.15 | | | |
| " | 4.10.15 | | A & B Companies relieved by C & D Companies | |
| " | 5.10.15 | | nothing to report | |
| " | 6.10.15 | | | |
| " | 7.10.15 | | C & D Companies left trenches | |
| " | 8.10.15 | | Proceeded by route march to AUBIGNY | |
| " | 9.10.15 1.30pm | | | |
| AUBIGNY | 10.10.15 | | | 13.10.15. 10 officers |
| " | 11.10.15 | | Battalion in Camp Training. Nothing to report. | Discharge transfers in 3 |
| " | 12.10.15 | | | |
| " | 13.10.15 | | | |
| " | 14.10.15 | | | |
| " | 15.10.15 | | | |
| " | 16.10.15 | | | |
| " | 17.10.15 | | | |
| " | 18.10.15 | | | |
| " | 19.10.15 | | | |
| " | 20.10.15 | | DENE | |
| " | 21.10.15 | | Major P., 2nd Batt. D.C.L.I., took over command of Battalion | |
| " | 22.10.15 9am | | Proceeded by route march to BERTANGLES. | |
| BERTANGLES | 23.10.15 | | nothing to report. | |
| " | 24.10.15 | | " | |
| " | 25.10.15 10.15a | | Proceeded by route march to VIGNACOURT. | MATTHEWS |
| " | 26.10.15 | | Notes by Bugler | |

Army Form C. 2118.

# WAR DIARY
## or
## INTELLIGENCE SUMMARY.

(Erase heading not required.)

Instructions regarding War Diaries and Intelligence Summaries are contained in F. S. Regs., Part II. and the Staff Manual respectively. Title pages will be prepared in manuscript.

| Place | Date | Hour | Summary of Events and Information | Remarks and references to Appendices |
|---|---|---|---|---|
| VIGNACOURT | 27.10.15 | | nothing to report | |
| " | 28.10.15 | | " | |
| " | 29.10.15 | | " | |
| " | 30.10.15 | | " | 30.10.15 by M [illeg.] |
| " | 31.10.15 | | " | |

2353  Wt. W2344/1454  700,000  5/15  D. D. & L.  A.D.S.S./Forms/C. 2118.

28 ½ Ber.

121/7608

36th Kivaim

7th Ox & Bucks L.I.
Vol I
Sept Oct 15

I. V.
9 sheet

Army Form C. 2118.

# WAR DIARY
## or
## INTELLIGENCE SUMMARY.
(Erase heading not required.)

M^h SERVICE B^n OXF and BUCKS L^T INF^TY.

| Place | Date | Hour | Summary of Events and Information | Remarks and references to Appendices |
|---|---|---|---|---|
| WARMINSTER | 19.9.15 | 1 AM | Advance party of all Regimental Transport (1st line and Train) together with machine gun sections and signallers — 3 Officers and 109 other ranks, under command of Major L. Wheeler, entrained for Southampton Docks and embarked in two different boats for Havre, disembarking and stayed at No 3 rest camp for about 28 hours, on 21st Sept^r entrained for Longeau - south east of Amiens and marched to billeting area (a distance of 14 miles) at Saleux where they joined the Battalion on the 23rd September 1915 | |

[signatures]

Army Form C. 2118

# WAR DIARY
## or
## INTELLIGENCE SUMMARY

4th Service Batt. Oxf/Bucks L.Inf.y

(Erase heading not required.)

Instructions regarding War Diaries and Intelligence Summaries are contained in F.S. Regs., Part II. and the Staff Manual respectively. Title Pages will be prepared in manuscript.

| Place | Date | Hour | Summary of Events and Information | Remarks and references to Appendices |
|---|---|---|---|---|
| WARMINSTER | 21.9.15 | 3 P.M. | The Battalion paraded for foreign service, strength, 26 officers & 881 other ranks, and entrained for Folkestone Harbour arriving at 10 P.M., and embarked for Boulogne, disembarked 1 A.M. 22nd and proceeded to Ostrohove rest camp. | |
| BOULOGNE | 22.9.15 | 2.30 A.M. | Entrained at Boulogne for Saleux, riding arriving at 9.15 P.M., detrained and marched to Briquemesnil and Saisseval for billets. | |
| BRIQUE-MESNIL & SAISSEVAL | 23.9.15 | — | General clean up and rest | |
| BRIQUE-MESNIL & SAISSEVAL | 24.9.15 | 9 A.M. | Paraded and marched to Ferrieres, and were inspected en route by General Sir Charles Munro, Commander of III New Army, after which they billeted in Ferrieres. | |
| FERRIERES | 25.9.15 | 7.30 A.M. | Paraded and marched 18 miles to Fouilloy, skirting Amiens; inspected by General Wilson, Commander XIIth Army Corps — billeted in Fouilloy | |
| FOUILLOY | 26.9.15 | | Cleaning up and rest. | |
| FOUILLOY | 27.9.15 | | Battalion training in neighbourhood | |
| FOUILLOY | 28.9.15 | | Battalion training in neighbourhood | |

Army Form C. 2118.

# WAR DIARY
## or
## INTELLIGENCE SUMMARY.
(Erase heading not required.)

4th SERVICE BN OXF AND BUCKS LT INFTY

| Place | Date | Hour | Summary of Events and Information | Remarks and references to Appendices |
|---|---|---|---|---|
| FOUILLOY | 29.9.15 | 9.30 AM | Paraded and marched to Meaulte and Becordel for billets — attached to 8th Infantry Brigade, 18th Division for instruction in Trench Warfare — half battalion being billeted in each village. Battalion Head Quarters at Meaulte. During the night 29-30 the billets of the half Battalion at Becordel were shelled, this being the first time the battalion came under fire. [signed] Capt & Adjt | |
| MEAULTE & BECORDEL | 30.9.15 | 3 PM | Officers and N.C.O's of 2 Platoons of each company proceeded to the trenches for 24 hours duties in trench warfare being attached to 6 North Staffs Regt & 12th Middlesex Regiment [signed] Capt & Adjt | |

[signatures] Lieut Colonel
Comdg 4 (S) Bn Oxf & Bucks L.I.

Army Form C. 2118.

# WAR DIARY
## or
## INTELLIGENCE SUMMARY
(Erase heading not required.)

4th SERVICE Bn OXFn BUCKS LI Nn FIFTY

| Place | Date | Hour | Summary of Events and Information | Remarks and references to Appendices |
|---|---|---|---|---|
| MEAULTE & BECORDEL | 1.10.15 | 3 P.M. | The Platoons (whose officers and N.C.O's were in Trenches) and Service Section, Machine Gunners under Lieut Skillet, went into Trenches for 48 hours duty, being attached to above mentioned Regiments. — Private Loude and Wootton of "D" Company were wounded during the night. — Remainder of Battalion at drill. | |
| — do — | 2.10.15 | 3 P.M. | Ditto — Corporal Stubbs, "A" Coy was killed, having volunteered to visit a post. Pte Mapley "D" Company, gassed by explosion of German mine. | |
| — do — | 3.10.15 | 3 P.M. | Above mentioned Platoons and Machine Gun Section returned to billets from Trenches, and Officers and N.C.O.s of remaining Platoons went to Trenches for 48 hours instruction. Remainder of Battalion at drill &c. | |
| — do — | 4.10.15 | 3 P.M. | Remainder of Platoons and Reserve Machine Gun Section under Lieut Raffle and 2nd Lieut Kerr, went into Trenches for 48 hours instruction. — Private Tooley of "B" Company was wounded during the night. | |
| — do — | 5.10.15 | 3 P.M. | Ditto. Private Baird of "B" Company was wounded during the night. | |
| — do — | 6.10.15 | 3 P.M. | Two platoons of "B" and two platoons of "D" Company evacuated Trenches at 3 P.M. The two remaining platoons of "A" & "C" Companies entered Trenches at 9 P.M. for 24 hours instruction as bombers — Machine gun section under Lieut Miller also went into the Trenches at 9 P.M. — Ten Rank & File were killed, and Two | |

Army Form C. 2118.

# WAR DIARY
## or
## INTELLIGENCE SUMMARY.
(Erase heading not required.)

4 OXFY BUCKS LT INFTY

| Place | Date | Hour | Summary of Events and Information | Remarks and references to Appendices |
|---|---|---|---|---|
| MEAULTE BECORDEL | Continued 6.10.15 | | All of whom belonged to No 1 Platoon of "A" Company — which was shelled by German trench mortars, whilst occupying a shelter; 2nd Lieut Manning was wounded whilst directing the rescue party, which excavated the men buried in debris of shelter. Gile Capt + Adjt | |
| -do- | 7.10.15 | 9 P.m. | "A" & "C" Companies and Machine Gun Section evacuated trenches at 9 P.m. "B"&"D" Companies and 1st Reserve Machine Gun Section entered trenches under Lieut Noble at 9 P.m. for 24 hours instruction. Gile Capt + Adjt | |
| -do- | 8.10.15 | 2 P.m. | "B"&"D" Companies and 1st Reserve Machine Gun Section evacuated trenches at 2 P.m. Private Beasley "B" Company was wounded, whilst in night by shrapnel, whilst in billet. Gile Capt + Adjt | |
| -do- | 9.10.15 | 9.30 am | Battalion paraded and marched to billet at FOUILLOY, rejoining 184th Infy Brigade and 26th Division. Gile Capt + Adjt | |
| FOUILLOY | 10.10.15 | | Battalion attended Divine Service, also were lectured on use of smoke helmets and all ranks walked through gas wave with smoke helmets on. Gile Capt + Adjt | |
| FOUILLOY | 11.10.15 | | Battalion Training in the vicinity of FOUILLOY. Gile Capt + Adjt | |

Army Form C. 2118.

# WAR DIARY
## or
## INTELLIGENCE SUMMARY.
(Erase heading not required.)

1/4 O&B OXF Y BUCKS LT INFTY

| Place | Date | Hour | Summary of Events and Information | Remarks and references to Appendices |
|---|---|---|---|---|
| FOUILLOY | 12.10.15 | | Battalion Training in neighbourhood of FOUILLOY | [signed] Capt Adjt |
| — do — | 13.10.15 | | — do — | [signed] Capt Adjt |
| — do — | 14.10.15 | | — do — | [signed] Capt Adjt |
| — do — | 15.10.15 | | — do — | [signed] Capt Adjt |
| — do — | 16.10.15 | | — do — | [signed] Capt Adjt |
| — do — | 17.10.15 | | The Battalion attended Divine Service — There was also a kit inspection and a general clean up. | [signed] Capt Adjt |
| — do — | 18 & 19 & 30th | | Battalion paraded and marched to LANEUVILLE for Camp. The Machine gun section (Service of 1st & 2nd Reserve Sections) remaining at FOUILLOY for instructing. The Battalion was attached to 27th Division | [signed] Capt Adjt |
| LANEUVILLE | 19.10.15 | | Battalion training in vicinity of LANEUVILLE | [signed] Capt Adjt |
| — do — | 20.10.15 | | Working parties at Trench digging. Remainder of Battalion at training in vicinity | [signed] Capt Adjt |
| — do — | 21.10.15 9.30am | | Battalion paraded and marched to FOUILLOY for Billets | [signed] Capt Adjt |
| FOUILLOY | 22.10 & 23rd | | Battalion paraded and marched with 4th Corps Troops to BERTANGLES for Billets | [signed] Capt Adjt |
| BERTANGLES | 25.10.15 | | Battalion Training in vicinity of BERTANGLES | [signed] Capt Adjt |

Army Form C. 2118.

# WAR DIARY
## or
## INTELLIGENCE SUMMARY.
*(Erase heading not required.)*

Instructions regarding War Diaries and Intelligence Summaries are contained in F.S. Regs., Part II. and the Staff Manual respectively. Title pages will be prepared in manuscript.

7'S/B OXF & BUCKS LT INFTY

| Place | Date | Hour | Summary of Events and Information | Remarks and references to Appendices |
|---|---|---|---|---|
| BERTANGLES | 24.10.15 | | Battalion training in vicinity of BERTANGLES. | Sd. Capt. Adjt |
| -do- | 25.10.15 | | Battalion attended Divine Service. Kit inspection and a general clean up. | Sd. Capt Adjt |
| -do- | 26.10.15 | | Battalion training in vicinity of BERTANGLES (Brigadier am) | Sd. Col & Adjt. |
| -do- | 27.10.15 | | -do- | Sd Capt Adjt |
| -do- | 28.10.15 | | -do- | Sd Capt Adjt |
| -do- | 29.10.15 | | Brigade Training (Trench warfare) | Sd. Capt Adjt. |
| -do- | 30.10.15 | | Bn training in vicinity of BERTANGLES | Sd. Capt Adjt. |
| -do- | 31.10.15 | | The Battalion attended Divine Service. Kit inspection and general clean up. 1 Sergeant 1 Corporal 1 Lee Corpl & 27 Pte arrived from England for posting to Battn. | Sd Capt Adjt |

J. Newton Lieut Colonel
Comdg 7'S/B Oxf & Bucks L.I.

Army Form C. 2118.

# WAR DIARY
or
## INTELLIGENCE SUMMARY.
(Erase heading not required.)

Summary of Events and Information

Men admitted to Hospital during Month of October.

| Place | Date | Hour | | | | Remarks and references to Appendices |
|---|---|---|---|---|---|---|
| | | | 9th.Glouc. Regt. | 11th.Worc.Regt. | 7th.Ox & Bucks L.I. | 7th.R.Berks Regt. |
| | | | 22 | 32 | 20 | 13 |

Sd. Thomson, Brit/Lieut
Comdt 7th & 9th Inft Bde
3.10.15 —

Appendix I

General Notes and Instructions as to Billeting area of 78th Infantry Brigade Group.

1. The 78th Infantry Brigade Group ( less 115th Bde R.F.A.& 204 Coy. A.S.C.) will be billeted to the west of Amiens as shown on map herewith AMIENS sheet 12.

2. The areas have been allotted as follows.

 H.Q. 78th Inf Bde & Signal Section Le Chateau FERRIERES.

 9th Glosters. Remainder of FERRIERES
          TOULAY FARM.

 11th Worcesters. FOURDRINOY
        RAMAIT FARM
        TEN FOL FARM

 7th OX & BUCKS L.I. BRIQUEMESNIL
         SAISSEVAL
         SAISSEMENT.

 7th Royal Berks. AILLY SUR SOMME from west end of village to where railway crosses road.

 78th Field Ambulance. Rest of AILLY SUR SOMME.

 108th Field Coy R.E. ST CHRIST Farm.

Note. H.Q. of 26th Division is at Le Chateau, GUIGNEMICOURT.

3. Protection. The area being out of the region of actual hostilities no question of protection arises.

4. Detraining Point. The detraining point for personnel is SALEUX, for animals and transport LONGEAU.

5. Route. The route each unit is to take to its area is shewn on map herewith AMIENS.S.O.12. As a help to units guides have been engaged to meet them, but they are not always reliable, and if they do not report, the map alone must be used.

6. Water on line of march. The only water on line of march is at SALEUX station for personnel, and for animals just outside LONGEAU station.

78/36 K Knaun

9th G'cedes vol I

12/7761

M.D.  I. L.
5 whole

Sept. 15 + OCT

Army Form C. 2118.

# WAR DIARY
## or
## INTELLIGENCE SUMMARY.
(Erase heading not required.)

Instructions regarding War Diaries and Intelligence Summaries are contained in F. S. Regs., Part II. and the Staff Manual respectively. Title pages will be prepared in manuscript.

| Place | Date | Hour | Summary of Events and Information | Remarks and references to Appendices |
|---|---|---|---|---|
| Sandhill Camp | 15.9.15 | | On this date Lt Col Churchill who had been found medically unfit for Active Service handed over command of the battalion to Major Joan. | |
| | | | Drafts to re-cast oversees were definitely received for the battalion to embark on the 20th Sept. but this order was cancelled subsequently and orders for the 21st substituted. | |
| | 19 | 10 a.m. | The Transport and advance body under Major J.D.J. Colet left Sandhill Camp and at 1.45 a.m. left Southampton by Rail for Southampton en-route for France. | |
| | 21 | | R.H. 21st the battalion in two halves, the 1st Commanded by Col 6.J.B. Wills and the second under Major J. Stonchele by Major Stonchele left Warmender Southampton embarking on the R.M.S. Queen. Gre. the battalion once joined by Major Stonchele had been on leave from 18th inst. | |
| | 22 | | The battalion arrived safely at Boulogne about midnight and marched to No 2 Base Rest Camp which lamp was left at 9 p.m. and the battalion entrained at Boulogne for Colincove from where it marched into Corcieux where billets were taken up and where the advanced party under Major Birdeys had already arrived. It is worth noting that there was not a single case of absence by the battalion when it left England. I was however called upon to find an escort for 19 absentees of the 97th Brigade. These absentees were | |
| | 23 | | handed over to the 97th Div. on the 23rd inst. About 10:30 a.m. an Air-ship was witnessed & German Air Craft being heavily shelled by Anti-Air-Craft Guns and also cloud by French By-Planes. | |
| | | | On the 20th inst. the billets at Corcieux were evacuated, and the Brigade marched on Amiens to Bruly, a distance of 18 miles. This distance was covered in 8 hours including halts. The Corps Commander saw the Brigade pass about a mile outside Aubigny and the following day on Orders complimented the battalion on its appearance after a trying march. | |
| | | | The 26th, 27th & 28th was devoted to battalion training and the repair of clothing and equipment. On the latter date Major J.R.H. Collis took over Command of the 26th Siv. Salvage Coy. Sery. Carried on by L. R. Smith Lt. M. Sloaner attached to that Company. | |

# WAR DIARY
## or
## INTELLIGENCE SUMMARY.
*(Erase heading not required.)*

Army Form C. 2118.

| Place | Date | Hour | Summary of Events and Information | Remarks and references to Appendices |
|---|---|---|---|---|
| | | | The billets at Lucilly were evacuated on the 28th Sept. and the battalion marched to Cappelly under orders for attachment to the 6th Division for instruction. | |
| | | | On the 29th inst. the battalion marched to Boescpe to relieve the "Queen Victoria Rifles", the Battn. remaining at Boesc-our-Someni. "A" & "B" Coys were accommodated in dugouts in Rifle Wood & "B" & "D" Coys in dug-outs at Kenny. | |
| | | | The hill casualties occurred on the 1st October. No Officers. "C" Company was killed by shrapnel and Capt. Waugh, "D" Coy received gunshot wounds in night attacks of 2nd/3rd Oct. At this date Lieut. & M. L. Fogler joined the battalion from Reserve & 2nd M. Trevelyan arrived from front accidentally unfit for Active Service prior to Embarkation. Capt. H. Pettoe also appeared in battalion orders as transferred to Reserve of Officers from 15th Sept. "B" & "D" Coys took over a portion of the 3/4 Trenches at 7.30 by Platoons & then by Companies for 48 hours. "A" & "C" Companies taking over for a similar period in the trenches to this date. | |
| | | | Lieut. R. L. M. Hope admitted to hospital. | |
| | | | The Battn. "C" Coy received a billet wound on the 8th inst. and died in hospital on the morning of the 9th inst. | |
| | | | The Kings Own Yorkshire Light Infantry relieved the battalion on the night of the 8th and march back to billets at Chisulty, the last Company arriving at 9am on the 9th inst. Leaving at 10 am on the 9th inst. the battalion marched back to Locality, taking up the billets accepted prior to leaving for Cappei. | |
| | | | On Sunday 10 Oct. the battalion marched through a cloud of gas the men wearing their new helmets. | |
| | | | Battalion Training was carried out on the 11th, 12th & 13th and on the 14th Oct. Light Infantry | |

Army Form C. 2118.

# WAR DIARY
## or
## INTELLIGENCE SUMMARY.
*(Erase heading not required.)*

Instructions regarding War Diaries and Intelligence Summaries are contained in F.S. Regs., Part II. and the Staff Manual respectively. Title pages will be prepared in manuscript.

| Place | Date | Hour | Summary of Events and Information | Remarks and references to Appendices |
|---|---|---|---|---|
| | | | The Adjutant Capt Molmon with an advanced party of 1 N.C.O. & men of "C" Company left Souilly at 5 a.m. to prepare a camp for the battalion in a wood near Mureaux, where it had been ordered for the purpose of preparing a second line of defence. 500 men daily being employed on this duty. Major J.D.J. Bishop & Capt W.H. Jeune were admitted to Hosp on the 19th and 9 on the 20th on the "C.C." the battalion returned to Souilly for the night. From Souilly the battalion marched to Mureaux-sur where was posted about 3-15 p.m. the march having taken 6¾ hrs. On the 24th Oct the 102nd French Mortar Battery consisting of 2 officers and 23 N.C.O.s men with two 2" French Mortars joined the Battalion. Lieut. L.E. McClintock was admitted to hospital on the 28th Oct suffering from rheumatism. | |

Jane, Lieut Col
Comdg. 9th (S) Bn GLOUCESTERSHIRE REGT.

# WAR DIARY or INTELLIGENCE SUMMARY.

Army Form C. 2118.

9th S Croydon Regt.
October 1915

| Place | Date | Hour | Summary of Events and Information | Remarks and references to Appendices |
|---|---|---|---|---|
| | 1 | | The first Supply arrived on October 1st when Bn began to be kitted by shipment and Sergt. Major's received Swords at night. On the same Lieut. J. Moore & Lepper joined the Battalion vice Lieut. O'Meara & Trevelyan who had been found medically unfit for active service prior to embarkation. Lieut. Allen received news of his promotion to rank of Captain on 10th September. | |
| | 2 | | On the night of 2nd October "C" & "D" Coys took over a portion of the front trenches at first by platoons & then by Companies for 48 hours. A & B Companies taking over for a similar period on 6th October. | |
| | 6 | | On the 6th October 2/Lt M.P. Grubb was admitted to hospital, the Battalion was relieved from the trenches by the Kingsown Yorkshire Light Infantry and marched back to CHIPILLY the last Company arriving at billets at 2 am on the 9th October. | |
| | 9 | | The Battalion paraded at 9 am on the 9th October and marched to FOUILLOY taking up the billets occupied prior to leaving for BRONFAY. | |
| | 10 | | On Sunday 10th October the Battalion was marched through a | |

Army Form C. 2118.

# WAR DIARY
## or
## INTELLIGENCE SUMMARY.
*(Erase heading not required.)*

G. Clarke
October 1915

| Place | Date | Hour | Summary of Events and Information | Remarks and references to Appendices |
|---|---|---|---|---|
| | 10 Oct | | Cloud of gas the men wearing their smoke helmets. | |
| | 11-14 | | Battalion training as usual and on the 11th 12th & 13th raids on the 14th October. Capt Pickells and the Adjutant Appleton with an advance party of 100 men left Fouilloy at 3 pm to prepare a camp for the battalion in a wood near MORCOURT where we had been ordered for the purpose of preparing a 2nd line of defence. 500 own orderly being employed on this duty. | |
| | 19 | | On the 19th October Major Booth and Capt Gramm were admitted to Hospital and on the 21st the battalion marched back to Villers au Fouilloy | |
| | 22 | | From Fouilloy the battalion marched into billets at MORTON VILLARS leaving Fouilloy at 6.30 am on the 22nd and arriving at 3.15 pm. | |
| | 24 | | On the 26th October the 10/25 Trench Mortar Battery assembly of 2 Officers & 23 NCOs & men with 2 Trench Mortars joined the Battalion. | |
| | 28 | | 2/Lieut F.E.M. CLARKE was admitted to hospital on the 28th Oct suffering from Appendicitis | |

J.D. I.M.

11/21/7431

Mr Kirwin

11th Wheeler
vol I of II

Sept & Oct 15.

Army Form C. 2118.

# WAR DIARY
## INTELLIGENCE SUMMARY.
(Erase heading not required.)

| Place | Date | Hour | Summary of Events and Information | Remarks and references to Appendices |
|---|---|---|---|---|
| | | | 11th (Service) Bn: The Worcestershire Regt. | |
| LONGBRIDGE DEVERIL. WILTS. | 19/9/15 | | The Bn: (except Machine Gun Section and all baggage) entrained at WARMINSTER and proceeded overseas via SOUTHAMPTON and disembarked at HAVRE, FRANCE, on 20.9.15 and proceeded to LONGUEAU (S.E. of AMIENS 2 miles) by train; thence they marched to FOURDRINOY (8 miles W. of AMIENS) and went into billets, arriving on 21.9.15. Strength of party:- 3 Officers, 109 other ranks:- Lt.Col. W.F. Barker, C.M.G. D.S.O. in Command. | Ref: M.f/s FRANCE - Sheet 12 AMIENS. |
| | 21/9/15 | | The Bn: (less party mentioned above, entrained at WARMINSTER in two trains and proceeded overseas via FOLKESTONE and disembarked | |
| FRANCE | | | at BOULOGNE, FRANCE, during night- 21/22.9.15. Strength of Bn: 27 Officers, 849 other ranks. Colonel T.M. Rainey - Robinson, C.B. in Command. | |
| | 22/9/15 | 12.32 pm | The Bn: went to Rest Camp at OSTROHOVE Camp (2½ miles N. of BOULOGNE) and then proceeded by rail to SALEUX (6 miles S.W. of AMIENS) and went into billets at FOURDRINOY. | - do - |
| FOURDRINOY | 24/9/15 | 10 am | The Bn: marched from FOURDRINOY to PONT-du-METZ (via FERRIERES) where it went | |
| PONT-du-METZ | | | into billet | |
| FOUILLOY | 25/9/15 | 9 am | The Bn: (in Bde:) marched from PONT-du-METZ to FOUILLOY (via AMIENS-LONGUEAU- | |

1577  Wt.W10791/1773  500,000  1/15  D.D. & L.  A.D.S.S./Forms/C. 2118.

Army Form C. 2118.

# WAR DIARY
## or
## INTELLIGENCE SUMMARY.
(Erase heading not required.)

Sheet 2

| Place | Date | Hour | Summary of Events and Information | Remarks and references to Appendices |
|---|---|---|---|---|
| FOUILLOY | 25/9/15 | | (AUBIGNY) where it went into billets. | Ref: map FRANCE - Sheet - 12. AMIENS. |
| " | 26.9.15 | | General mustering up in billets. | |
| " | 27.9.15 | | Bn: training on ground just E. of FOUILLOY. | |
| " | 28.9.15 | | Bn: training on ground just E. of FOUILLOY. | |
| SAILLY LORETTE | 29.9.15 | 10 a.m. | The Bn: marched from FOUILLOY to SAILLY LORETTE (via CORBIE - VAUX-SUR-SOMME - SAILLY-LE-SEC) where it went into billets. Orders were received that the Bn: would be attached to the 14/Bde: (5/Divn) for instruction in Trench Routine. | |
| | 30.9.15 | 3.30 p.m. | "A" & "B" Coys: and Service Maxim Machine Gun. proceeded to SUZANNE for attachment to 5/Cheshires (T.F.) and 1/D.C.L.I. for instruction in the trenches. | |

30/9/15

A.M.Rainey-Robinson Colonel.
Comdg: 11/Northd R.

Army Form C. 2118.

Page 3.

# WAR DIARY
## or
## INTELLIGENCE SUMMARY
(Erase heading not required.)

| Place | Date | Hour | Summary of Events and Information | Remarks and references to Appendices |
|---|---|---|---|---|
| MARICOURT and SUZANNE | 1st to 8th Oct. 1915 | | From the 1st to 8th Oct: 1915, the Bn: was attached to the 1/D.C.L.I. and 1/Cheshire R. for instruction in trench duties and routine. The instruction consisted of the following:- <br><br> (A) 24 hours attachment of individual Officers and N.C.O's. These were attached to Coys: of the above units who were occupying the fire trench in their respective sectors and accompanied Officers and N.C.O's holding corresponding positions to learn their particular work. <br><br> (B) 48 hours as platoons. Platoons were attached to Coys: in the fire trench and formed part of those Coys: for the time being. By this means all ranks saw the details of trench routine and how the various duties were carried out. | Ref. Map. FRANCE. Sheet 12. AMIENS. |

Army Form C. 2118.

Page 4.

# WAR DIARY
## or
## INTELLIGENCE SUMMARY.
(Erase heading not required.)

| Place | Date | Hour | Summary of Events and Information | Remarks and references to Appendices |
|---|---|---|---|---|
| MARICOURT and SUZANNE | 1st to 8th Oct 1915 | | (c) 24 hours no Conflict: Companies. During this period "A" Coy: of the Bn: to which our Coy: were attached withdrew from the fire trench and one of our Coy: took over a Coy: sector and carried out all duties and routine for that sector. During the attachment two Coys: moved between SUZANNE and MARICOURT as required. The following casualties occured during the attachment:— — WOUNDED — Lieut. J.R.T. Marsham — on 4.10.15. by shrapnel — serious. Capt. A.A. Downe — on 2.10.15. by rifle grenade — serious. No: 10916 Pot. E. Battle — on 4.10.15 — by shrapnel — slight. No: 16098  "    J. Tyndon — on 4.10.15 — by shrapnel — slight. No: 16115 | Ref. Map FRANCE Sheet 12 A.M.12.V.8 |

Army Form C. 2118.

Page 5.

# WAR DIARY
## or
## INTELLIGENCE SUMMARY.
(Erase heading not required.)

| Place | Date | Hour | Summary of Events and Information | Remarks and references to Appendices |
|---|---|---|---|---|
| SUZANNE | 7.10.15 | 6 p.m. | On 7th Oct. "A" & "B" Coys. under the Command of Lt. Colonel W.F. Barker, C.M.G. D.S.O. marched from SUZANNE to SAILLY LORETTE where they went into billets. | Ref. Map FRANCE. Sheet 12 |
| SAILLY LORETTE | 8.10.15 | 6 p.m. | H.Q. "C" & "D" Coys. under the Command of Colonel R.M. Rainey-Robinson. C.B. marched from SUZANNE to SAILLY LORETTE where they went into billets. Thus bringing the whole of the Bn. together again. | A.M. 12 N'S. |
| FOUILLOY | 9.10.15 | 10 a.m. | The Bn. marched from SAILLY LORETTE to FOUILLOY where it went into the billets. it paraded on 29th Sept. 1915. | |
| | 10.10.15 | | Battalion training on ground just E. of FOUILLOY | |
| | 11.10.15 | | do | |
| | 12.10.15 | | do | |
| | 13.10.15 | | do | |
| | 14.10.15 | | do | |
| | 15.10.15 | | do | |
| | 16.10.15 | | do | |

Army Form C. 2118.

Page 4.

# WAR DIARY
## or
## INTELLIGENCE SUMMARY.

(Erase heading not required.)

| Place | Date | Hour | Summary of Events and Information | Remarks and references to Appendices |
|---|---|---|---|---|
| FOUILLOY | 16/10/18 | | On this date the Bn. was organised into 5 Coys. the 5th Coy: being the H.Q. Coy: which was composed of all Bn. H.Q. details such as :- Machine Gun Section, Grenadier Coy:, Signallers, Transport Establishment, Pioneers, Police Army Room Clerks, and Q.M. establishment. Coys. were also designated by numbers on this date, is under :-<br>"A" Coy: numbered No: 1 Coy.<br>"B" " " " 2 "<br>"C" " " " 3 "<br>"D" " " " 4 "<br>"E" " " " 5 " | Ref. Map.<br>FRANCE.<br>Sheet 17.<br>AMIENS. |
| | | 7.15 p.m. | Orders were received today that the Bn. would march tomorrow to FRAMERVILLE (H.Q. & No: 1 & 2 Coys.) and VAUVILLERS (Nos. 3 & 4 Coys.) for attachment to the 32nd Division for the purpose of working on the 2nd line of trenches. | |
| FRAMERVILLE<br>&<br>VAUVILLERS | 18/10/18 | 9.30 a.m. | The 1st Bn. marches from FOUILLOY to FRAMERVILLE and VAUVILLERS. | |

Army Form C. 2118.

Page 4

# WAR DIARY
## or
## INTELLIGENCE SUMMARY.
*(Erase heading not required.)*

Instructions regarding War Diaries and Intelligence Summaries are contained in F. S. Regs., Part II. and the Staff Manual respectively. Title pages will be prepared in manuscript.

| Place | Date | Hour | Summary of Events and Information | Remarks and references to Appendices |
|---|---|---|---|---|
| | | | | Ref. Map FRANCE Sheet 12 AMIENS. |
| FRAMERVILLE & VAUVILLERS | 19/8/15 | | (via WARFUSÉE - ABANCOURT) where it went under canvas. Coys. worked under the supervision of R.E. on 2nd line trenches about RAINCOURT - FRAMERVILLE and VAUVILLERS. |  |
| | 20/8/15 | | Work on 2nd line trenches. An urgent message was received this afternoon ordering the Bn. back to hills of FOUILLOY. |  |
| | 21/8/15 9.30am. | | The Bn. returned to FOUILLOY where it was ascertained that Major General Wilson, 13th Corps. Commander, was going to SERVIA with this Division, our Division (26th) not being one of them. To-day we also learnt that the whole of the 26/Div: was to be attached to the 10th Corps, while the 10th Corps was being re-organised. Consequently the 26th Division received orders to move int. hills in the village about 5 to 6 miles N. of AMIENS. |  |
| VAUX-EN-AMIENOIS | 22/8/15. Sun. | | The Bn. (in Brig.) marched from FOUILLOY to VAUX-EN-AMIENOIS (5 miles N. of AMIENS) via CORBIE - PONT NOYELLES - QUERRIEUX - |  |

1577  Wt.W10791/1773  500,000  1/15  D.D.&L.  A.D.S.S./Forms/C. 2118.

Army Form C. 2118.

Page 5

# WAR DIARY
# or
# INTELLIGENCE SUMMARY.

(Erase heading not required.)

| Place | Date | Hour | Summary of Events and Information | Remarks and references to Appendices |
|---|---|---|---|---|
| VAUX-en- AMIENOIS | 22/10/15 | | ALLONVILLE — COISY — BERTANGLES, where it went into billets, other Coys. of the Bn. went into billets in villages nearby. | Ref. Map FRANCE Sheet 12 AMIENS. |
| | 23/10/15 | | Bn. Training on Ground just N. of VAUX-en-AMIENOIS. | |
| | 24/10/15 | | Church parade and remaining up in billets | |
| | 25/10/15 | 8.30 a.m | At 8.30 a.m this morning a message was received from Bde: H.Q. ordering the 78/Bn. to be on the Bn. Alarm Post at 11 a.m. The information was communicated to all concerned at once and the Bn. arrived at the Bn. Alarm Post complete in every detail at 10.30 a.m. At 11 a.m. the Brigadier informed the C.O. that it was a practice alarm and the Bn. returned to billets at VAUX-en-AMIENOIS | |
| | 26/10/15 | | Bn. Training on Ground around VAUX-en-AMIENOIS | |
| | 27/10/15 | | do | |
| | 28/10/15 | | do | |
| | 29/10/15 | | do | |
| | 30/10/15 | | Bde. Training (ATTACK) on Ground N. of FREMONT. | |

Army Form C. 2118.

Page 9

# WAR DIARY
## or
## INTELLIGENCE SUMMARY.

(Erase heading not required.)

| Place | Date | Hour | Summary of Events and Information | Remarks and references to Appendices |
|---|---|---|---|---|
| VAUX-en-AMIENOIS | 31/10/15 | | Church parade and mustering up in billets. | Ref Map. FRANCE Sheet 12. AMIENS. |

McHairy-Robins Colonel
Comdg 11/Royal R